BRUSH!

By Jodi Rawlinson

Library For All Ltd.

Brush!

First published 2022

Published by Library For All Ltd
Email: info@libraryforall.org
URL: libraryforall.org

Our Yarning logo design by Jason Lee, Bidjipidji Art

Original illustrations by Angharad Neal-Williams

Brush!
Rawlinson, Jodi
ISBN: 978-1-922951-71-7
SKU01398

BRUSH!

Ouch!

Mum, my teeth hurt!

Off to the dentist
we go.

If you don't brush,
germs will grow.

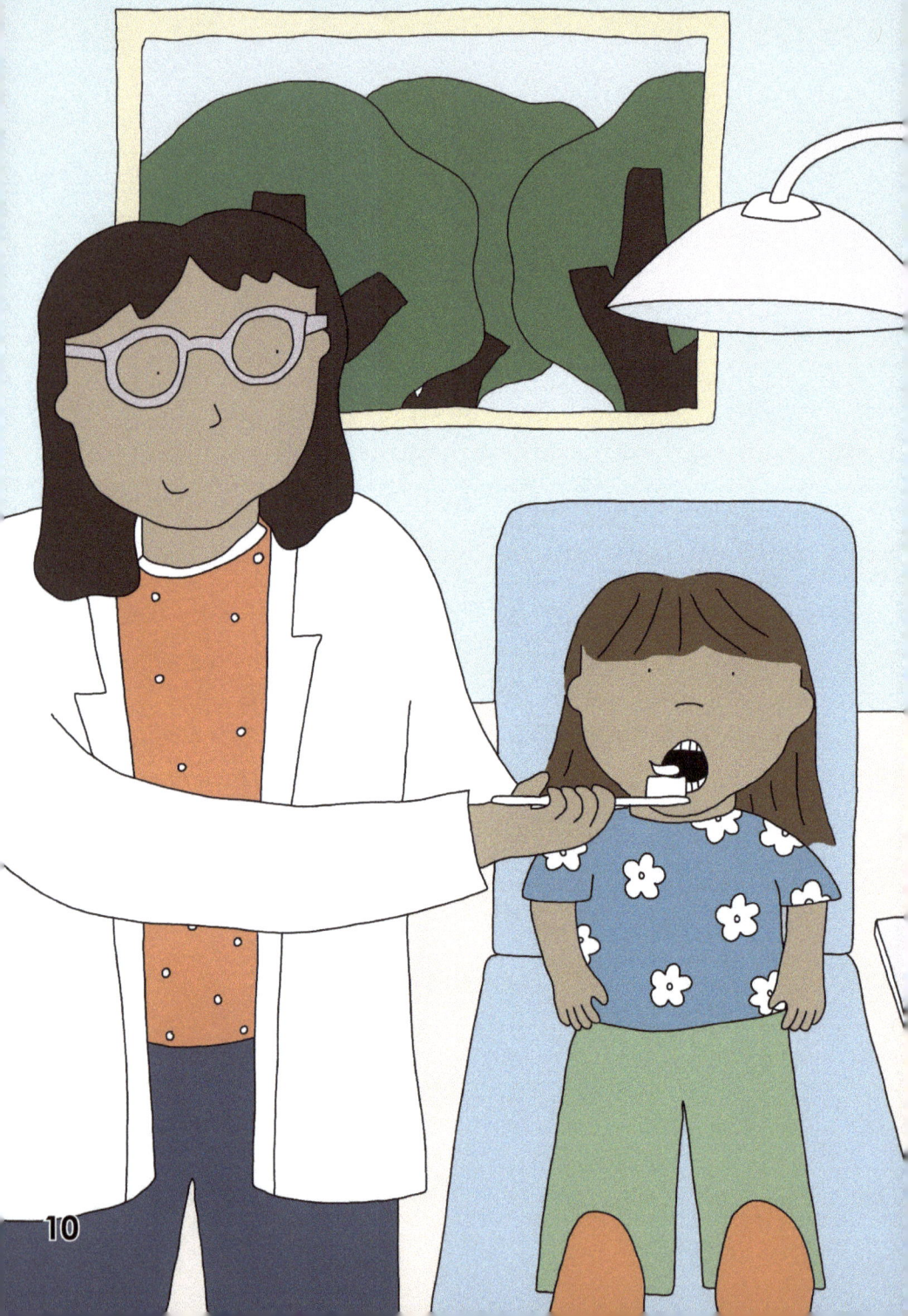

Let me show you,
then you know.

Brush

Rinse

Spit

I know I can do it!

Come here, Tayla.

DENTIST

18

All clean!

You can use these questions to talk about this book with your family, friends and teachers.

What did you learn from this book?

Describe this book in one word. Funny? Scary? Colourful? Interesting?

How did this book make you feel when you finished reading it?

What was your favourite part of this book?

download our reader app
getlibraryforall.org

About the author

Jodi was born in Adelaide and is from the Arrernte, Warlpirri and Torres Strait Islander Nations. She lives in Canberra and loves gardening and reading. When Jodi was younger, she loved reading *Alice in Wonderland.*

Our Yarning

Want to discover more books from this collection? Our Yarning is a collection of books written by Aboriginal and Torres Strait Islander peoples across Australia.

We know that children learn better, and enjoy reading more, when they see themselves in the stories, characters and illustrations of the books they read.

To download the app, visit the Google Play Store on any Android device and search 'Our Yarning'.

libraryforall.org

www.ingramcontent.com/pod-product-compliance
Lightning Source LLC
Chambersburg PA
CBHW042346040426
42448CB00019B/3424